BYNV HEBREW ROOTS
DICTIONARY

Hebrew Transliterations & Definitions for BYNV

The Besorah of Yahusha Natsarim Version

This is a partial listing of Hebrew / Eberith transliterations of words used in the <u>BYNV</u> with definitions. Meanings are determined by the *context* of the word. How a word is used in a sentence helps us discern how to apply a proper definition. In English, *pitcher* can mean more than one thing, and Hebrew words can have more than one meaning too. At the end of this glossary is a *letter comparison chart*. The **context** supplies a word's meaning in a sentence. A common error of many students and teachers is to consult a concordance and select a definition on a whim. The meaning of a word must not be applied without mindfully taking the context into account.

Compiled by Lew White

BYNV HEBREW ROOTS DICTIONARY

This is prepared for the English-speaking reader who is motivated to pronounce the Name of our Creator, and many of His other words as accurately as possible without the influences of human alterations.

It is based on the letters as written, and is a labor of love. The word *Hebrew* gets its origin from one of Abrahim's ancestors, Eber. All descendants of Abrahim are therefore also Eberim (the plural form). Abrahim the Eberi was given a name meaning father of nations, and his seed has been mixed among all the people of the Earth to one degree or another due to the scattering of the tribes.
Arabs who descend from Abrahim's first-born male child are also Eberim, naming their children many Hebrew names, such as Yusef, Miryam, Yaqub, Daud, and many others. Other cultures and languages have contributed to the distortion of the **sound** of the original speech over time. Scripture calls the language spoken by the Eberim **Yahudith** (see H3066; YashaYahu / Isaiah 36:13 in an interlinear translation).

CONTENTS

Ab, Abba [alef-beth] .... Father, male head of household, strong protector

Aban [alef-beth-nun] .... stone

Abrahim .... *Father of nations*; male parent of Yitshaq (Isaac), grandfather of Yaqub (Jacob).
Origin name Abram, renamed by Yahuah: Abrahim - father of Guyim or father of multitudes

Adam .... Man, mankind, human, humanity, Earthling; created with a shared essence / character with Yahuah, in order to **rule over** creation; depending on the context, it can also mean red, or soil

Adun, Aduni .... My sovereign, my lord, or my master. Commonly seen as *Adonai* due to vowel additions by Masoretes after 8th century CE/AD

Afraim .... Second son of Yusef, received blessing of first-born. His name means *fruitful.* Commonly spelled *Ephraim*

Al, Alah .... Al, Alah, Alahim are pronouns meaning the mighty, high, or *lofty one*. The plural ending can refer to the size, overwhelming majesty, enormity, or power of the One Who is lofty, and may apply to the quality, not the quantity. In other cases, the plural *"other alahim"* is referring to the many false mighty ones worshipped by the heathen. Commonly we see the spelling **El, Eli,** or **Elohim** due to the subtle distortion of vowels invented by the *Masoretes,* Karaite **traditionalists.** The first letter is **ALEF**; an **A**, not an **E**. Al is pronounced *ALL*. Yahuah has hidden the sound

4

of His original Speech in a most unexpected place: Arabic-Hebrew.

Those who are concerned that EL, and ALAH have been used as **proper nouns** by pagans should distinguish the difference between a **NAME**, and a **clean Hebrew word** that is a **pronoun**. Other cultures have picked up many clean Hebrew words and turned them into names, such as Aman, Adon, and Molok. When not used as **names**, these terms are authentic, clean words.

The decendants of Abrahim through Yishmaal (Arabs) were not attacked and carried into all the world. They continue **to utter the old form** of many Hebrew (Yahudith) words. The Arabs are Eberim, **Hebrews,** being descended from Abrahim.

They refer to their mighty-one as **allah**, which they know is not a name, but simply means lofty one or a *god*, as they explain it to English-speaking people today. The term ALAH **is original**; but **their** allah is not **our Alah, Yahuah**, since **their** allah does not have a son, and they do not obey Yahuah's Covenant of love. Many other words are preserved on their lips. Arabic-Hebrew (from *the other side of the family*) preserves the original sound of words such as *Abram, Daud, Yusef, Yaqub, Aishah, Adam, Iason,* etc. The Arabic/Hebrew word for mother, *um*, closely resembles the modern Hebrew *em* [vowel-trouble again]. The Arabic/Hebrew for father, *ab*, is more correct than the modern Hebrew, *av*, since there was not a letter **V** in ancient Hebrew (Eberith, and later referred to as Yahudith).

Am, Ama [alef-mem] Mother, female term, one giving birth, nurturer; EM [ayin-mem] means *people.* AM means *mother*

Aman .... 3 Hebrew letters, alef-mem-nun: **AMN** [AMAN] Meaning: affirmation; *truly, trusted, affirmed, believe, confirm* The femine form is **amanah**, found in Scripture translations as belief, but means trustworthy. Both aman and amanah refer to the idea of being **trustworthy** and **truthful**.

It is perfected or shown by **action**, the active belief expressed outwardly. *"Who has believed our report?"* [YashaYahu 53:1] The word believed uses this root AMN to convey belief, and that **belief** is perfected only by **obedience**.

The affirmation of our amanah (belief in, or integrity) is shown in our behavior, or how we live it out. If we do not live by the Word we claim to believe, our belief is dead. We show our *belief* by our *works*, the way we live, approved by the Word of Yahuah. Without obedience our belief is dead. This is the fruit of Yahusha who dwells in us, giving us His Mind. The word AMAN is **not in any way** related to the Egyptian deity AMEN or AMON RA. The word **AMON** is the **Greek form** of the Egyptian word *YAMANU*, which meant the *hidden-one*.

There is no relationship or contextual connection between the Hebrew use of the word **AMAN** with the Greek or Egyptian languages. People are hearing things that aren't there, therefore they are being deluded / mesmerized by malicious teachings. Proverbs 14:15 tells us how a simpleton believes everything he hears, but a prudent person watches over their steps.

Arets .... Earth, soil, land. The "whole arets" refers to the entire Earth as we know it.

Amus .... The prophet (Amos); carried

Aish, Ashah ... Man, Woman - male: *aish*; female: *ashah*

Aramith .... The script and / or language of the Aramaeans, decendants of Aram, a people that occupied Syria, Assyria, and the land of Babel. The word *Aramith* is contrasted with **Yahudith** *(the name of the language spoken by the Eberim)* in Scripture *(see an interlinear to verify at YashaYahu / Isaiah 36).* The conversation at the wall of Yerushalim with the Rabshakeh of Sennacherib will show there was a distinction made between **Aramith** and **Yahudith** (see more details under *Eberith* below).

Asherah ... tree idol; the plural is Asherim. Seen today in the Christmas tree, a phallus depicting gonads (orbs) and semen (tinsel). The wreaths are the ancient symbols of the birth canal. The fertility symbols are camouflaged so the exoteric (outsider view) of the symbols of all Sun worship conceals the esoteric (insider view). Paul knew about the concealed **fertility symbols**, and he wrote that it is shameful even to mention what the disobedient do in secret.
At Ephesians 5, Paul was speaking to these former pagans, and teaching them to obey Turah, and stay away from their former **weak and miserable principles** (Galatians 4).
As their bunny baskets and Christmas trees defile them, we Natsarim are attempting to show them a better way to walk before the wrath of Yahuah is poured out full strength.

Astoreth ... plural of Astoreth, Philistine deity; aka Astarte; equivalent to Eostre, Eastre, Easter, Isis, Ishtar, and others.

Baal, BEL …. Lord, Aduni, owner; a word adopted as a proper noun (name) for the Kanaanite storm deity BEL, in Hebrew it is spelled BETH-AYIN-LAMED plural: **Belim**

Barashith …. Often, the first word or phrase is the name for the books of Scripture. Barashith means **in the beginning.** The root is RASH; **BA** (in) + **RASH** (head, beginning) + **ITH** The plural ending *ITH* implies the *quality* of importance, size, or overall magnitude of the thing described, not *quantity*.
The Greek name for this book: *Genesis*

Behemah …. A beast, living creature; plural: *BEHEMOTH* The plural may refer to a single beast of a great size. Certain plural endings in Hebrew pertain to quantity, but in some cases the quality of strength or size. Also used as a metaphor for the principalities controlling and ruling mankind (clergy, nobility, and laity), given power and authority by the dragon. A more modern term is **beast**: a giant monster (World Order).

Beital …. Bethel, meaning **house of AL**

BYNV …. *Besorah of Yahusha Natsarim Version*

Besorah …. Message, testimony, report

Danial …. My judge is Al

Eber …. The ancestor of Abrahim. Eber's name means *over*, cross-over, or other-side. He is the ancestor of the

tribes of Yisharal (Israel), and Yishmaal (Ishmael, the Arabs).
Eberim is the plural form. Eber's name gives us today's terms Hebrew, and Hebrews.

Eberith .... *The script and / or language of the Eberim.* The script and language is commonly called *Hebrew* today. Hebrew speech is called **Yahudith*** (see interlinear text at YashaYahu / Isaiah 36).
*H3066: YAHUDITH

Farah .... [pe-resh-ayin-hay] usually seen as the Greek form, *Pharaoh*, a title for the ruler of Mitsrim (Egypt). The word means *great house* in the Egyptian language. This political and religious ruler was believed to be a deity, Horus, the son of Osiris. These reflect patterns adopted from Babel where Tammuz was the son of Nimrod, who was believed to be the "son of the Sun." It explains how people believed in reincarnation, and Egypt's fascination with embalming mummies, and equipping them for their passage into the next world.

Farat .... A river commonly known by its Greek form, Euphrates

First-fruits .... This is a shadow or outline using the waving of barley during the week of Matsah, or Unleavened Bread. Following Passover, we see the sign of Yunah because Yahusha's resurrection is the redemptive shadow showing Him to be the First-fruits. It's really not about barley at all, the barley was simply the shadow; Yahusha's resurrection is the reality.

Guyim …. Plural form of guy, meaning Guyim, Guyim. The word means nation or nations, often referring to the foriegners we are commissioned to teach the Name of Yahuah and His Covenant. Those responding will engraft to Yisharal by pledging themselves to the Covenant in immersion; then they are to be treated the same as native-born. There is no dividing wall; the same Turah applies to all.

Hekal …. Temple, Shrine *The House built by Shalomoh, destroyed by Babylonians, rebuilt after return from Babel under governor, NekemYah*

Kanukah …. Dedication (aka Chanukah, Hanukkah)

Kerem …. Vine, vineyard, or garden
The Hebrew word for vineyard is *KEREM*. This word is spelled with three letters in the original Eberith (Hebrew) script: KAF – RESH – MEM (please see letter chart on last page) Yahusha is the KEREM (Vine), and we are His NATSARIM meaning *branches, watchmen, or guardians*

Kodesh …. Renewed month, cycle, *period of time* (see QODESH)

Kohen …. Hebrew word for priest; plural *kohenim* The meaning is friend, worker, minister, server. Cognate words include kahuna, kahin, king, koehn, kohn, cohn; revealing how the word is synonymous with many statements about us becoming kings and priests under Yahusha, our Kohen haGadol (the High Priest)

Kuram-Abi: [2 Kron 2:13] ,,,, *A Tyrain man of the tribe of* **Dan** *filled with wisdom and skill. In their drive to promote Reason as the highest goal, modern Masonry's Adepts refer to this man as they seek vengeance against 3 allegorical conspirators they claim slew Huram: government, religion, and private property – Marxist philosophy embracing Secular Humanism, situation ethics, athieism, and communism [New World Order, New Age, the worship of Reason]*

Lailah …. Night, darkness

Lui …. The name of the father of the tribe of priests, *Lui*; plural form *Luim*, commonly seen as LEVI, LEVITE; Aharon and Mosheh were *Luim*

Malakim …. Messengers; singular form: malak, "angel"

Mayim …. Water, waters; a component of **shamayim**

Miqara …. Proclamation; root *QARA*, to proclaim, or call. MIQARA is another phonetic spelling, seen as UYIQARA, *"and he called."* The **Karaites** derive their name from the meaning. The Arabic term **quran** is derived from the Hebrew word **qara**.

Mishkan .. Temple, Dwelling Place

Moad …. Appointment; plural form: moedim

Molok …. Kananim / Muabim deity also known as Rephan, Kemosh [to Amonites], Kiun, Tophet, etc.,. Children were offered alive to **pass through the fire** as offerings to this abomination. Sitting in Santa's lap is an echo of this practice.

December 25th is the approximate time of the winter solstice, when the Sun began to return northward again. All the pagans' names for their Sun deities were babbled forms of the original solar deity, Nimrod. Molok, Ra, Zeus, Ahura Mazda, Mithras, Apollo, and dozens of other names are occult references to Nimrod, *who is Santa, the first superman.*

Even the superman logo is a serpent.

Santa/Molok and all his trappings, *(flying beasts bringing gifts to place under the tree, his Asherah),* are all used to teach little children the ways of the devil.

Pastors know these things, but are silent about them, as millions pass into eternity and never hear the Truth.

Musheh …. Hebrew spelling: mem-shin-hay: *draw-out*

Nekemyah .... *Yahuah consoles*, the post-captivity governor of Yerushalim given authority to rebuild the Mishkan (dwelling place, Temple) and walls of the city.

Nashim .... Wives

Natsarim .... Plural for Natsar. The original followers of Yahusha were the *sect of the Natsarim* (Acts 24:5). The word means *watchmen, guardians*, also *branches*.
We are branches of the teachings of the Root.
"I am the Vine; you are the Natsarim." - Yn. 15:5
Join a community of us: **www.natsarimlife.com**

Nazir .... An oath of separation for a specific purpose and duration. It also refers to the person under the oath. This is an entirely different word than Natsar.

Nefesh .... Breath, blast, living spirit, life-giving essence, cognate with nehash (breathe), and nekash (hiss). Often translated *soul,* inner being, strong man, psyche.

Qodesh .... Peculiar, special, precious, exceptional, distinctive, treasured above all, esteemed. (not KODESH, the word for month)

Rab, Rabbi .... Chief; rabbi means *my chief,* or *my exalted one.* The Rabshakah (chief of the princes) mentioned at 2 Kings 18:17 was an Assyrian official sent against Yerushalim, also mentioned at YashaYahu chapters 36 & 37.
We have no chief but Yahusha.

Ruach ... Breath, wind, breeze, also known as spirit

Sefer .... a *book* (Latinized form: cepher)

Shabath [shin-beth-tau] . . . rest, cease, complete shalom, the 7th day of each week, a sign forever between Yahuah and His people. It is the test given by Yahuah to determine who will obey Him, and is the sign of the eternal Covenant.

Shabathuth .... Plural form of shabua: *weeks*. The event memorialized as the marriage Covenant between Yahuah and Yisharal. The Eternal Covenant is annually observed on the 50th day after First-fruits, and is always on the first day of the week, the *"morrow after the seventh Shabath"*

Shalomoh .... Peaceful, Man of peace, son of Daud

Shabua .... Week, from root *sheba*, seven; plural form: *Shabuoth* (weeks)

Shamash .... Servant; context may refer to the visible object called the Sun, or the adopted name for the deity pagans called on to worship the Sun. The context supplies a word's intended meaning in a sentence. A common error of many students and teachers is to consult a concordance, and select a definition on a whim. The meanings a word may have must not be applied mindlessly without discerning the context.

Shamayim .... Skies, heavens. The word means lofty, and the second part of the word refers to "waters" – the waters from which all creation began with.

14

Shaul .... Usually seen as SHEOL; Abode of the dead, **the grave**, commonly called hell, meaning *hole* - not the same as the Lake of Fire, **Yam Aish.** The same Hebrew letters [shin-alef-uau-lamed] also spell a word sounding the same (a homonym), Shaul. The context of will identify it as a proper noun (name). Shaul was the 1st king of Yisharal, whose name means *asked for.* Although words may be spelled and sound exactly alike, we must use their *context* to determine what they mean in a sentence.

Shamar .... *Watch, guard.* We often see the idea softened to the English word, *keep.* It includes the concept of hearing and obeying carefully, to heed. We guard and watch over Yahuah's Torah carefully, we don't just *keep* Torah. Shamar is the root for the area called Samaria (more accurately, Shamarun, where northern tribes built fake Temple for worship). The tob Shamaruni (the good Samaritan) guarded the life of the man in the parable told by Yahusha.

Shamarun .... Known as Samaria, a hill in the northern area of the land used as a watch station. The word is based on the word *shamar, to watch or guard.* The father of Ahab, Amri (Omri) built it up, establishing a dynasty of kings to rule the northern tribes of Yisharal.

Sukah, Sukuth .... Shelter, shelters, temporary dwellings

Sus .... Hebrew spelling *samek-uau-samek* – meaning *horse*

Talmid .... Student, pupil; plural form, *talmidim*

Turah .... Instruction; plural form *Turoth*

Tsabauth .... Armies; *tsaba* (army) + plural suffix, *uth*

Tsedek .... Upright, obedient, righteous. Tsedekah is obedience in practice, literally the living-out of the Word of Yahuah.

Tsitsith .... Tassels (purplish-blue in color, see Num. 15, Dt. 22). They are worn on our garments to remind us to obey the instructions of Torah always. The Hebrew word also applies to the place on a plant where fruit will appear, the *tsits*, meaning **blossom.**

Tsiun .... Literally, the location of the City of Daud. Usually spelled Zion, Sion, or Tsiyon. The meaning is signpost, from the verb root *tsuh*, command or charge. Tsiun is the place of authority from which the ruler of Yisharal is identified to reside, and possesses authority to dispense the full code of law.

Uriyah .... [commonly read as Uriah] *Yahuah is my Light.*

Yahuah .... 4 vowels: **yod-hay-uau-hay**. The Personal Name of our Creator, meaning: I will be, *I was, I am, I will be.*
Used 6,823 times in the TaNaK, but replaced by translators with other words meaning "lord" across the languages; Aduni (Eberith), Kyrios (Greek), Dominus (Latin), and LORD (Anglican / English).
Greek word, *Tetragrammaton*, means 4 letters.

Yahudith .... This word is a transliteration indicating the **name of the language** spoken by the Eberim living in

Yerushalim, as distinguished from the Assyrians who spoke Aramith. James Strong documented the word Yahudith as H3066, and it is spelled **yod-hay-uau-daleth-tau**.
An interlinear Hebrew-English translation will show this at YashaYahu / Isaiah 36:13. (I mention this on the back cover)

Yahusha .... Name of Mashiak, means: *Yah* (I am) *your Deliverer. In a dream, this is the Name the messenger told Yusef to call the Mashiak.* The assistant of Mushah was *Husha,* and was renamed *Yahusha* (Numbers 13:16). Husha means *deliverer,* hay-uau-shin-ayin.
Yahusha means *I am your Deliverer,* yod-hay-uau-shin-ayin.

Yam, Yamim .... Lake, sea; *yamim:* seas

Yam Aish ... Lake of fire, place of permanent, utter destruction; this is the second death

YashaYahu .... *Deliverer is Yahuah;* known as *ISAIAH,* his name is an inversion of the name YAHUSHA. The first three letters yod-shin-ayin (YASHA) are rendered ISA in Greek and Latin. The IAH is YAH, also shared in other Hebrew names.

Yekezqal .... *Al strengthens;* this prophet known today as *Ezekiel* was given prophetic insights concerning the scattering and eventual regathering of the tribes of Yisharal.

Yerak .... *Moon* (the visible object, the Moon) Yereku is the city people today call *Jericho,* named after this Hebrew word for the **Moon**.

YirmeYahu .... *Yahuah uplifts;* the prophet called
Jeremiah

Yisharal .... *Ruler with Alahim;* **Shar** means prince, ruler;
seen today in terms such as sheriff, sharif. The word is built
around the root **shar**, with the single letter **yod** as a prefix,
and the **al** as a suffix: Y (to) + SHAR (rule) + AL (Alahim)
means *to rule with Alahim.* It is not Yasharal, since
YASHAR means upright, straight, on-the-level, or honest.
Word roots are getting mixed by teachers doing shallow
research.
This elect group is often referred to in Scripture as the
bride, or ashah, of Yahuah, the one body in Covenant with
Him, into which foreigners **must graft in**, or perish without
any hope.
(see YashaYahu / Isaiah 56)
All who accept the Renewed Covenant through the covering
of Yahusha's blood (trusting in His offering, not the blood of
animals), must be **immersed** as the outward sign of their
pledge / commitment to obedience. Their obedience is the
sign that Yahusha has circumcised their mind with a love for
His Covenant, now written on their heart. This seals them
as Yahusha's elect for the Day of the redemption of their
bodies. By learning Yahuah's Covenant of love, every
person is convicted of transgressing His instructions.
Yahusha's perfect offering of His own blood redeems
completely. There remains to more offering for sins (see
Eberim / Hebrews 10).
The hand-writing that was against us is wiped clean (the list
of our sins). They are forgotten, and His blood redeems us.
Through the process of being convicted in our heart that we
need Him, we repent (turn back), and pledge to obey

Yahuah's instructions in His power as we call on the Name of Deliverance for the forgiveness of sin: Yahusha. He is our Rock and our Redeemer.

Yom, Yomim … Day, days; it is often and exact measurement of a night/day cycle, but the context may express figurative meaning, as "in those days," or when the Sun rises. Sunset is the end of each "day," and a new one begins in darkness, as it was in the beginning on the first day. "There was evening (darkness), and there was morning (boker), the first day."

Yusef …. Son of Yaqub, father of Afraim (Ephraim) & Menashah; distorted by letters & vowels of gentile languages to become "Joseph"

Zunah …. Whore, cult / shrine prostitute

"This is written for a generation to come so a people to be created praise Yah." Tehillim - Psalms 102:18

**Repent - for the Reign of Yahuah draws near!
The Message** (Besorah) **of Yahusha; did you hear it?**

HOW HEBREW CHANGED

Names, scripts, and the way they sound changed in many ways over the last two millennia.

If you desire to know the facts and will do the research, it will be apparent that the Hebrew teachers are using a foreign script carried-back from the captivity in Babel. To add insult to injury, that *script* was further maligned in the 8th century CE by a Qaraite sect called the Masoretes (meaning "tradition" from MASORAH).

REJECTED STONE: THE NAME

STONE FOUND IN SHOMERON

The majority of the alterations of Hebrew names and words seem to come after the 8th century CE as the phonetic cues were invented by the Masoretes.

The little twiddlydiddles are called niqqud marks, causing a reader of the Name of Yahuah to say another word, *"adonai."*

MASORETIC VOWELS

ARAMAIC LETTERS WITH NIQQUD MARKS
THIS IS NOT HEBREW
TORAH INSTITUTE

These marks are not found prior to the 8th century CE.
The Dead Sea Scrolls are over 1000 years earlier than the Masoretic scriptures, and have no such marks.

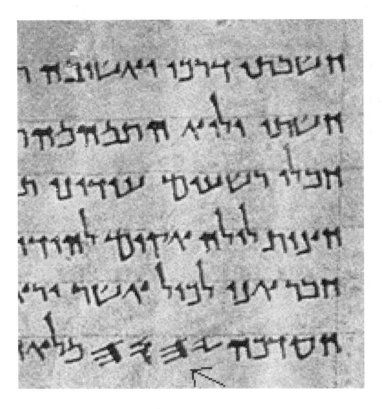

By the time the printing press was invented in 1450 CE, the English colonies were being established. By 1611, the next big thing occurred; many of the world's language groups began to learn to speak the English language by reading the Anglican Catholic Authorized Version taught by missionaries. This (the KJV) was based on the Latin Vulgate translation by Eusebius Hieronymus Sophronius (Jerome) used for over 1200 years previously.

James Strong compiled his concordance by 1890 based on the KJV, filling the world with teachers trained by the influences of the niqqud marks invented by the Masoretes. (YAHU became YEHO)

Although Strong attempted to transliterate the Name of Yahuah, he landed on JEHOVAH due to the Masoretes. In the 1700's, the J sounded like a Y.

The inherited tradition of deleting the Name of Yahuah from subsequent translations is now beyond being conspicuous. It was replaced by *LORD*.
Many odd spellings emerged for the Name of Yahusha over the centuries, some referred to as **Christograms.**
The Septuagint's Greek form ignored the Eberith phonology and gave us IESOUS. Capitalizing the IES we see it became IHS. This form was adopted by the western empire (IHS).
Another christogram was used by the eastern empire, IC-XC.
Later corrupted forms developed such as IESV, IESVS, JESUS, and ISA.

BARUK HABA BASHEM YAHUAH
NATSARIMLIFE.COM
JOIN US AT THE LINK ABOVE

ABOUT VESSELS & WINE

OLD WINE:
The teachings of men are traditions inherited passed-down over generations. These man-made customs commonly dominate behavior, taking precedent over the Words we are to live by written by the Creator. They are a heavy burden we can remove easily by choosing to stop listening to them, recognizing their teachings are nothing to Yahuah; they are only arrogant nonsense someone made up for people to follow. The old wine is the **leaven** of men's teachings.
We must be strong and courageous, and obey Yahuah.
It's a choice between their teaching authority, or Yahuah's.
NEW WINE: The teachings of Yahusha, without human traditions mixed in. New wine is pure Truth, and cannot be in the presence of old wine. The old wine will conflict **with the new, having the excuse "The old is good enough."**

WINESKIN: The heart, mind, or inner person that receives teachings, accepting both Truth and error based on personal choices. A renewing of this mind, or wineskin, is given when a person **surrenders** their mind, along with the old wine, to Yahusha. The new wine would burst the old wineskin, and cannot be in the presence of the old wine. The wineskin is the receptacle, or vessel, we call our mind. It is our inner heart. Unrenewed by the Ruach of Yahusha, it is a mind of the flesh. A mind of the flesh does not, and cannot, obey, and repels pure Truth (the new wine). Receiving the Mind of the Ruach, one's vessel (wineskin) understands the Scriptures, and the will of Yahusha, so the person pants to obey, knowing the thoughts of Yahusha. They have received a love for the Truth, and their hearts (wineskins) are circumcised by Yahusha. They see the world and its condition, and sin, for what they are in Yahusha's perspective. Yahusha has given them His Mind, and they see everything as He does.

HOW TO GRAFT-IN
IMMERSION IS YOUR PLEDGE
Immersion is our outward sign of a good conscience toward Yahuah, and our "dipping" (baptein) represents our **circumcision**; carefully notice Kol. 2:11,12:
"In Him you were also circumcised, in the putting off of the sinful character, <u>not</u> with a circumcision done by the hands of men, but with the circumcision done by Mashiak, having been buried with Him in immersion (baptism) **and raised with Him through your belief in the power of Yahuah Who raised Him from the dead."**
An infant cannot possibly be considered capable of knowing what is happening. Immersion is an act of your own personal will; You covenant personally with Yahusha, and it

24

is your **heart** (inner spirit, the seat of your will) that He circumcises with a **love** for His Turah. Our immersion is the moment we personally enter into the renewed Covenant with Yahusha, our Maker, when **He** writes His Turah on our hearts, explained at Jer. 31:31-33, and quoted at Hebrews chapters 8 & 10. It's operation is explained in Romans chapters 6,7, & 8. We become a citizen of the commonwealth of Yisharal. According to Rev. 12 & Rev. 14, we are sealed in His Name, and enjoin to Yahuah as a member of the sect of the **NATSARIM** (see Acts 24:5, 28:22), the **first-fruits**. We are those who do 2 things: we obey the **Turah,** Commands of Yahuah, and hold to the Testimony of Yahusha. His Natsarim are guardians or watchmen, and we guard His **Name** and His **Word**.

OUR PLEDGE IS A CHOICE between LIFE & DEATH
Dt. 30:19 & 1Yn 5:11-13:
**"And this is the witness: that Alahim has given us everlasting life, and this life is in His Son. He who possesses the Son possesses life, he who does not possess the Son of Alahim does not possess life.
I have written this to you who believe in the Name of the Son of Alahim, so that you know that you possess everlasting life, and so that you believe in the Name of the Son of Alahim."**
Yahusha circumcises our hearts (minds) Kol. 2:11-13:
"In Him you were also circumcised with a circumcision NOT MADE WITH HANDS, in the putting off of the body of the sins of the flesh, by THE CIRCUMCISION OF MESSIAH, having been buried with Him in IMMERSION, in which you also were raised with Him through the belief in the working of Alahim, who raised Him from

the dead. And you, being dead in your offenses and the uncircumcision of your flesh, He has made alive together with Him, having forgiven you all offenses."
The act of immersion is evidence of our circumcision, the outward sign or act of our belief, indicating the **circumcision** (cutting) **of our heart**. Men boasting in one anothers' flesh are missing the point. If we have received Yahusha's Ruach, we are His, and **He** has circumcised our hearts with a love for the Truth, a love for His **Turah**. If you have been circumcised with a circumcision not made with hands, you're done.

Nothing **you** can do can improve on what Yahusha has done. This is how we can "obey from the heart." When we love Him enough to obey Him, He will write His Turah on our hearts. Those who will not obey Him will not receive His Ruach (Acts 5:32).

"He who turns away his ear from hearing the Turah, even his prayer is an abomination." Proverbs 28:9.

The Turah (Word of instruction) is oil, also called living water. It is the MIND of Yahuah (His **will** living in us). It is the Mind of **the Ruach** of Yahusha, often called the Spirit. The Turah is inseparable from the Spirit of Yahusha, and it is **"living and active"** (Heb 4). Our heart is our **lamp**, the component within each of us (often called our mind). Our **heart** is what needs the **Living Words** to be poured into them, like **lamp oil** to our **lamp**, or **new wine** for our **new wineskin**. Stephen called the Turah given at Sinai the **Living Words**. Most reject them because they are guided by malicious shepherds, ravening wolves, masquerading as messengers of light.

"Listen to Me, you who know obedience, a people in whose heart is My Turah; do not fear the reproach of men, nor be afraid of their insults."
See YashaYahu / Is. 51:7.

PLEDGE OF A GOOD CONSCIENCE

Acts 5:32 tells us the Spirit of Yahusha is **only given to those who obey Him**; that means they turn and obey, and live in His Word, the Ten Commandments.

When going to steeples, were you ever trained to obey the Ten Commandments? Those who do not have Yahusha's Spirit in them cannot obey without Him, nor do they desire to do so. This is why so few people can receive His Spirit: They are taught to *disobey*. The translations they use were made by men who did not have Yahusha's Spirit in them because they did not obey the Ten Commandments.

1 Yn. 2:4 proves this. Revelation 22:14 reveals to us how those who do His Commandments will have the right to eat from the tree of life, and enter the gates into the city. Outside are the dogs. Are you ready to obey, and call on the Name of Yahusha for the forgiveness of your sins?

1Pet. 3:15-22:

"But set apart Yahuah Alahim in your hearts, and always be ready to give an answer to everyone asking you a reason concerning the expectation that is in you, with meekness and fear, having a good conscience, so that when they speak against you as doers of evil, those who falsely accuse your good behavior in Mashiak, shall be ashamed. For it is better, if it is the desire of Alahim, to suffer for doing good than for doing evil. Because even Mashiak once suffered for

sins, the obedient for the unobedient, to bring you to Alahim, having been put to death indeed in flesh but made alive in the Ruach, in which also He went and proclaimed to the ruachs in prison, who were disobedient at one time when the patience of Alahim waited in the days of Noah, while the ark was being prepared, in which a few, that is, eight beings, were saved through water, which figure *(example)* now also saves us: immersion – not a putting away of the filth of the flesh, but the pledge of a good conscience toward Alahim – through the resurrection of Yahusha Mashiak, Who, having gone into heaven, is at the right hand of Yahuah, messengers and authorities and powers having been subjected to Him."

CAN WE PERFORM OUR OWN PLEDGE ALONE?

Yes, we can, because all that matters is that Yahusha hears our words. Nicolaitanes don't like this, so most people are baptized into a denomination, and the only one that utters a word is the malicious shepherd dipping the person into the water. We can use any body of water; an ocean, stream, lake, pool, or bathtub. An elder is not **required** to be present, and if one is, it is only what we utter that matters. Don't worry, there *are* **witnesses***;* an abundance of *rejoicing* **malakim** (messengers). Our immersion represents the death of our old self and its inclination (character). We cannot clean-up or improve ourselves, but rather we acknowledge our filth and sin to the only One that can take our burden away forever, and *change our heart*. We go to Him broken-hearted and humble, and accept the cleansing of His perfect blood to cover our sins against His Covenant. Belief is shown by our obedience.

28

Heb 11:6: *"But without belief it is impossible to please Him, for he who comes to Alahim has to believe that He is, and that He is a rewarder of those who earnestly seek Him."*

First, we must believe that He **exists**, and we must know that "sin" is any transgression against His Turah (1 Yn 3:4). Admiting that we have transgressed against Him, we turn-back (repent) with all our heart and pledge to *obey* (stop sinning). We are now ready to enter into His Covenant, which is a **relationship**, not a religion. We go to the water to identify with Him in His death, burial, and resurrection from the dead. We pronounce our belief in His atonement for our sins through His shed blood (the perfect offering for sins), and **call** upon His **Name** for our deliverance. We accept with a love for His Turah (Truth, His Covenant), and **promise to obey Him as would a bride her husband** - Read YirmeYahu 31, Heb 8, Heb 10. We accept His love, and give Him *our* love; and this is love:

2Yn 1:6: *"And this is love, that we walk according to His commands. This is the command, that as you have heard from the beginning, you should walk in it."*

Acts 4:12 *"And there is no deliverance in anyone else, for there is no other Name under the heaven given among men by which we need to be saved."*

The Name given to all mankind for deliverance is **Yahusha**, meaning "I am your Deliverer." The *Name*, not the *Names*, indicates that it is Yahuah that became flesh, becoming our Deliverer, and the Name Yahusha identifies Him in the role of Deliverer, giving all honor to Yahuah in the Name of Yahusha as Deliverer (see Phil. 2).

Mat 28:18-20: ***"And Yahusha came up and spoke to them, saying, 'All authority has been given to Me in Heaven and on Earth. Therefore, go and make talmidim of all the guyim, immersing them in the <u>Name</u> of the Father and of the Son and of the Qodesh Spirit, teaching them to guard all that I have commanded you. And see, I am with you always, until the end of the age.' Aman."***

With each immersion, Yisharal increases in number. You may have been formerly Gentile, but after immersion you are no longer *gentile* (guyim: the nations).

Read Eph 2:11, and all of Eph 2 & 3, in context.

Exo 12:49: ***"There is one Turah for the native-born and for the stranger who sojourns among you."***

Once immersed, we are no longer strangers or foreigners, but **adopted children**. When we read the 10 Commandments, we should feel convicted of sin; we then repent by choosing to live by them, accepting the Covenant by being immersed. We are then sealed for the day of our redemption because we call on Yahusha's Name, and walk in obedience in His power.

TRANSLITERATIONS

	6,823	216	2	1
	YAHUAH	YAHUSHA	YAHUSHUA	Y'SHUA
HEBREW	𐤉𐤄𐤅𐤄	𐤉𐤄𐤅𐤔𐤏	𐤉𐤄𐤅𐤔𐤅𐤏	𐤉𐤔𐤅𐤏
ARAMAIC	יהוה	יהושע	יהושוע	ישוע
GREEK	IAOUE	IHSOUS		
LATIN	IEHOUAH	IESU		

AT HEBREWS 4 AND ACTS 7 THE SAME GREEK LETTERING IS USED FOR "JOSHUA" AND "JESUS" - IHSOUS

THIS IS CONFIRMATION BOTH WERE CALLED YAHUSHA IN HEBREW

TORAH INSTITUTE

The translation with the restored Name and phonetically clear transliterations of the Hebrew words in this glossary is pictured above, and available from amazon.com.

*"This is written for a generation to come,
so a people to be created praise Yah."*
Tehillim – Psalms 102:18

REPENT
[Reverse your direction]
for the Reign of Yahuahdraws near!

The Message (Besorah) **of Yahusha; did you hear it?**

Millions of families have been feeding on myths and lies mixed with Scripture for their entire lives, and those teaching them are paid to teach them. Those teachers will remain just as deceived as they have been, unless they go to them and ask them the questions found in this little book. None of the questions in this book will harm the Truth, but any one of them will destroy the lie that has been used to conceal the Truth. With the armor of Yahuah, and the fruits of the Living Alahim Who dwells in your mind, you may remain confident and assured that you are firmly established on the Rock of our deliverance. If you are not immersed and have never called on the Name of Yahusha for the forgiveness of your crimes against Him, you are not wearing the armor of Yahusha, and cannot bear the work ahead of you.

Take the first step, by studying the Ten Commandments. They will show you they are His seeds of the coming reign of Yahusha, and teach us all how to love Him and one another.

THIS IS THE LOVE
"For this is the love for Yahuah, that we guard His Commands, and His Commands are not difficult, because everyone having been begotten of Yahuah

32

overcomes the world. And this is the overcoming that has overcome the world: our belief. Who is the one who overcomes the world but he who believes that Yahusha is the Son of Yahuah? This is the One that came by water and blood: Yahusha Mashiak, not only by water, but by water and blood. And it is the Ruach who bears witness, because the Ruach is the Truth."
1 Yn. 5:3-6 BYNV

IMMERSION IS YOUR PLEDGE

Admit you have broken this eternal Covenant, and pledge to obey His Word from this point on. As you enter into a body of water, tell Him you will obey His Word, and trust in His perfect blood to cover your transgressions, the blood of the Lamb of Yahuah. Immerse completely, calling on His Name to deliver you, and you give your life to Him as His servant forever.

He will help you by writing a love for His Covenant on your heart (mind), enabling you to see the ugliness of rebellion as He does. Yahusha means, "I AM YOUR DELIVER."

COVENANT OF LOVE

1
I AM YAHUAH YOUR ALAHIM
HAVE NO OTHER BEFORE MY FACE

2
YOU DO NOT BOW TO IMAGES

3
YOU DO NOT CAST THE NAME OF
YAHUAH YOUR ALAHIM TO RUIN

4
REMEMBER SHABATH
GUARD IT AS QODESH

5
RESPECT YOUR FATHER & MOTHER

6
YOU DO NOT MURDER

7
YOU DO NOT BREAK WEDLOCK

8
YOU DO NOT STEAL

9
YOU DO NOT BEAR A MALICIOUS
WITNESS AGAINST YOUR NEIGHBOR

10
YOU DO NOT COVET YOUR
NEIGHBOR'S WIFE, HOUSE, FIELD,
SERVANTS, ANIMALS, OR ANYTHING
BELONGING TO YOUR NEIGHBOR

𐤉𐤄𐤅𐤄

I AM YAHUAH, THAT IS MY NAME
LOVE ME AND GUARD MY COMMANDS
LOVE YOUR NEIGHBOR AS YOURSELF
LOVE ONE ANOTHER AS I HAVE LOVED YOU

TORAHZONE.NET LAMBLEGACYFOUNDATION.COM   NATSARIMSEARCH.COM

The Ten Words above are to become your character because they embody the personality of Yahuah. He ordered us to teach them diligently to our children. The 4th one is the outward sign of the day of rest each week, showing we do not buy and sell on that day, or the 7 festival days we rest from work.

QUESTION: Why do the people who love Yahuah and obey His Torah suffer so much? Kefa (Peter) 5:8-10 explains this. Another answer is found at Revelation 12:17.

All things work together for good for those who love Yahuah and are called according to His purpose (Romans 8:28). The experience of Ayub (Job) tested the character of everyone around him. The world is filled with comfortable people, and unless they are challenged by pain, persecution, and loss, they would never turn to Yahuah or develop compassion and love. If we suffer, we are being refined and perfected, and to test the hearts of many who may have caused that suffering. All who suffer share in Yahusha's suffering, and YashaYahu 53 describes why the innocent suffer for the guilty. Ecclesiastes is another resource with great wisdom. In the end we are all tested in this mortal life to see if we will obey Yahuah, or place our trust in men. Pledge your life to obeying Yahuah, and He will give you His seal of ownership, and you will see what Psalm 91 means.

TURNING ASIDE TO MYTHS HAPPENS
WHAT COULD POSSIBLY GO WRONG?
CAUSE: 2 TIM 4   EFFECT: MAL 4   FOSSILIZEDCUSTOMS.COM

Merchants And Their Witchcraft

Acts 20:28 says the Ruach ha Qodesh shed His own blood to purchase (redeem completely) us. The Spirit of Yahusha indwells those who obey Him (Acts 5:32).

We call on our Creator as our deliverer by calling Him Yahusha. He is Yahuah, and as our Deliverer we use the suffix SHA at the end of the Name to refer to Him. If we do not obey His Commandments, we do not belong to Him, nor can we claim to know Him (see 1 Yn. 2:4).

The old traditions of men are as chaff, and the dragon

35

is enraged because people are turning back to obedience to the Commandments of Yahuah, repenting because they are sobering-up from the leaven of men's teachings: Sun-day; holy water, statues; replaced name; sacraments; praying to the dead / necromancy; special days they made up as "holy" yet not mentioned by Yahuah; teaching Yahuah's Word, but putting it behind them and not doing His Word; building steeples on every corner in spite of Uyiqara / Lev. 26:1, objects Yahuah hates; always learning, but never able to come to a knowledge of the Truth. Our teachers have led us into confusion. Yahuah our Alahim is One (Dt. 6:4); not three persons – that's Hinduism's influence on mankind, as well as the "4 – levels of interpretation" people keep hearing from teachers. Idolatry drives the economy of the world, just look at the seasonal displays of the merchants, and how silent the pastors are as they struggle to make them relevant with 3-point sophistry. Rebellion is as witchcraft, unrecognized by the simple; but the obedient watches his steps.

IDOLATRY

MANKIND'S MOST PROMINENT ACTIVITY

MANKIND'S DEFINITION
Extreme admiration, love, or revering of something or someone; worship of a physical object or person;

YAHUAH'S DEFINITION
Setting one's thoughts or actions on anything above Yahuah. He gives an example for us from His prophets, such as YashaYahu (Isaiah) 44:16.

IDOL EXAMPLES: politicians / rulers; movie or music idols; statues, pillars, toasting with drinks; prayers to any entities other than Yahuah, spirits, dead people (necromancy, beads).

IDOLATRY
MANKIND'S MOST PROMINENT ACTIVITY

Expressions we hear used all the time in conversations, and the things we run out to buy and decorate with show how invested we are in all the witchcraft, and hardly ever associate them with idolatry: rosaries, steeples horseshoes and rabbits' feet for good luck - bringing trees into our homes to celebrate a birthday, Black F-day, "let's keep our fingers crossed," horoscopes, palmistry, fortune cookies, baking cakes for birthdays, cone hats, toasting, blowing-out candles, wishes, eggs in baskets and rabbits in the spring, sunrise services, giving candy to costumed children on the day of the dead, Valentine's Day gifts, cards, hearts, and using decorations that remind everyone that we encourage the idolatry that drives the world's economy. The golden cup of Babel has caused madness!

DRIVING THE WORLD ECONOMY

Every merchant prospers from the fertility celebrations that hardly anyone perceives because they are all hypnotized from a lifetime of exposure to the traditions handed-down from our fathers to children. **Idolatry** is exactly what Yahusha referred to as *stumbling blocks* at Mt. 18:3-8. Idolatry is taught to children, and passes into each new generation through family bonding.

Yahuah is sending the plagues now, but most people remain clueless to why. Revelation 9:20 "And the rest of mankind, who were not killed by these plagues, did not repent of the works of their hands, that they should not worship the demons, and idols of gold, and of silver, and of brass, and of stone, and of wood, which are neither able to see, nor to hear, nor to walk. Merchants exploit the wormwood that causes the masses to stay drunk on the idolatrous fertility traditions.

Words have the power of life and death in them. Words of death often flow from the unredeemed, and even from those who have not walked with Yahusha very long. The longer you walk with Him, the more you become like Him. He is not cruel, so we are not cruel. We can't force love because it is a fruit, not a seed. It comes from Him, the Life of the Root. His life grows and bears His fruit in us. Love cannot be faked, but cruelty is easily seen as the fruit coming from the wicked treasure. Patience and compassion, and above all forgiveness, are expressed in all those who know Yahusha. The mark of the beast can be solved if you have wisdom (Torah).

Revelation 13 is a riddle, and all you have to do is understand what day you cannot buy or sell. The lie has been there all along, and all you need is wisdom to see it. When you receive wisdom, you can see everything as Yahusha does. Are you one us yet?

QUESTION: What is the greatest lesson to learn?
To love Yahuah, and love your neighbor. His Commandments are the seed, and when that seed grows, His fruit is seen in us. Life has no meaning higher than this purpose.

TEACH THEM TO YOUR CHILDREN & GRANDCHILDREN

QUESTION: How do we learn how to love?
Study diligently, and teach everyone around you, *to receive a love for the Ten Commandments.* Without these, the enemy has you **completely disarmed** in this spiritual war.

The dragon has made these illegal because all who **obey** them become the enemy. The knowledge of the Truth destroys the lie. Revelation 22 tells us those obeying the Commandments will have the right to the tree of life.

This may be the reason pastors keep away from teaching from the book of Revelation. You might understand it, and obey the Ten Commandments!

"Yahuah, my strength and my stronghold and my refuge,
in the yom of distress the gentiles shall come to You from the ends of the arets and say, 'Our fathers have inherited only falsehood, futility, and there is no value in them.'"

YirmeYahu / Jeremiah 16:19 BYNV

"And besides these, my son, be warned – the making of many books has no end, and much study is a wearying of the flesh. Let us hear the conclusion of the entire matter: Fear Alahim and guard His Commands, for this applies to all mankind! For Alahim shall bring every work into right-ruling, including all that is hidden, whether good or whether evil." Qoheleth / Ecclesiastes 12:12-14

If only you had obeyed My Commands!
YashaYahu / Isaiah 48:18

We will not see Him again until we say:

BARUK HABA BASHEM YAHUAH

BLESSED IS HE WHO COMES IN THE NAME OF YAHUAH – Psalm 118:26
See also YashaYahu (Isaiah) 25:9

How is the BYNV different from other familiar translations?

The following four photos will explain some of those differences.

BESORAH of YAHUSHA
NATSARIM VERSION

THE FAMINE
OF YAHUAH'S WORD
IS OVER

NO MORE
HIDING HIS IDENTITY

OUR DELIVERER'S NAME
IS ON THE COVER

WHAT THE TEXT
LOOKS LIKE:

Mt. 26:17
EVIDENCE
OF CONFUSION

PASSOVER: 14th

THE 1ST DAY
OF UNLEAVENED
BREAD IS THE
15TH

Have you ever heard someone say,
"I just don't understand what I'm reading?"
People are searching for the Heart of Yahusha,
but in most translations there are dispensational and
Masoretic distortions that block understanding because
His heart was not in the translator(s).
Respectfully, ignorance of Torah has blocked the under-
standing of both the translators and their readers.
Footnotes often argue with the text, steering a reader's
heart away from receiving the pure and simple instruc-
tions to live by. **They are ever learning, but unable to
come to a knowledge of the Truth.**
Truth was distorted, causing a famine of His Words.
We Natsarim love Yahusha's **Word**, and His **Name**.
The message (**besorah**) of the reign of Yahuah is pour-
ing forth into the world through His Natsarim. In this
Natsarim Version, all the blockages to the Truth are re-
moved. The One we **obey** is the one we **serve**.
A servant's **behavior** displays the will of their master.
Our heart is focused on Yahusha's instructions:
His **Torah** (this is **wisdom**, our **treasure**).

For those curious about readability, here is a sample of
the actual text, showing the font style and size:

TEHILLIM - PSALMS 23

₁ ꜰYꜰꝪ is my Shepherd; nothing do I need. ₂He makes me to
lie down in green pastures; He leads me beside still mayim.
₃He returns my breath; He leads me in paths of righteousness
for His Name's sake. ₄When I walk through the valley of the
shadow of death, I fear no evil. For You are with me; Your rod
and Your staff, they comfort me. ₅You spread before me a ta-
ble in the face of my enemies; You have anointed my head with
oil; My cup overflows. ₆Only goodness and lovingkindness follow me All the Yomim of my life; And I shall dwell in the House
of Yahuah, for the duration of Yomim! (Glossary defines terms)

Open your favorite translation to Mt. 26:17 and check
something right now, if you can. If it says "On the
first day of Unleavened Bread," then that translation
used the **KJV** as the primary blueprint to build on, and
failed to catch certain errors. The NIV back-pedals the
error at Mt. 26:17 in the footnotes. The Greek text has no

BYNV: Besorah Of Yahusha Natsarim Version
An English translation of all 66 books with the restored palaeo-Hebrew Names
Yahuah: ꜰYꜰꝪ   Yahusha: OWYꜰꝪ

(BYNV tract, page 1 of 4)

word "day" in the sentence, and the word "protos" indicates *"prior to"* Unleavened Bread. One cannot prepare for the Passover on the "first day of Unleavened Bread." The Greek text has the word *protos*, meaning something is *"near to, before, or prior to."* If one has a *"proto-cancer"* cell, it is **not yet** cancer, but getting there. The festivals of Yisharal were not familiar to Christian translators; but they are to Natsarim. This translation puts many details right, making pure Truth (new wine) easy to absorb into your renewed wineskin (renewed heart).

THE MESSAGE
COMES THROUGH
VERY CLEARLY

TRADITION: A stumbling-block, and when defended, it is also a **stronghold**. The teachings of **men** are "old wine", but the Truth is "new wine." The new and the old cannot be in the presence of the other. Doctrines of men have resided in hearts (old wineskins) for millennia. A renewal of hearts and minds (wineskins) must take place in order to receive the new wine. It's our training that matters. Even **our speech** needs to have things restored that have been hidden from us. Luke 12:2, 3:

"And whatever is concealed shall be revealed, and whatever is hidden shall be known. So, whatever you have said in the dark shall be heard in the light, and what you have spoken in the ear in inner rooms shall be proclaimed on the housetops."
We know the Name has been hidden: Proverbs 30:4:
"Who has gone up to the shamayim and come down? Who has gathered the wind in His fists? Who has bound the waters in a garment? Who established all the ends of the arets? **What is His Name**, And **what is His Son's Name**, If you know it?" ZekarYah 3 states His Name for all to see.

YAHUSHA IS
ALIVE, AND IN
HIS NATSARIM

People are unaware of things carefully planned behind closed doors. The **Masoretes** (traditionalists) invented "vowel-points" to supposedly "lock" the Hebrew words into a uniform pronunciation. *They worked at this from the 7th to the 11th centuries.* Their true agenda was to alter the **vowels** in words so the true pronunciation would be concealed. Notice again, Yahusha's Words above; He refers to something "hidden" that is not "heard", until it is "proclaimed". We see immediately how this would apply to the Name, **Yahuah**. The Name is the **Stone** the builders rejected, and has become the chief cornerstone. Ps 118
The Name is restored in this version, and there are many other restored words to stretch your renewed wineskin. For example, the word "**elohim**" as traditionally understood, should begin with the letter "a", ALEF. Thanks to the Masoretes, the true letter, "a", is not seen or heard. The true Hebrew word? **ALAHIM**. The first reaction is, *"Uh-oh, did I hear ALAH in there?"* This *pronoun*, which

THE NAME: THE STONE
THE BUILDERS REJECT

(BYNV tract, page 2 of 4)

is not a name, is more correctly pronounced by Arabs (who _are_ Hebrews) than the modern Yahudim. We have to distinguish their **religion** from their **language** in this case; Abraham knew Yahuah by His Name, but also as Al Shaddai. I've had to accept the Truth of all this, and not ignore it.

It's a simple **vowel-correction** throughout this version. Alef-Lamed is AL, not EL. Working closely with the Hebrew **without the influences** of the Masoretes' agenda restores the **pure lip**.

Yahudim today say AV & EM for father and mother; Arabs say AB & UM. Arabs name their children Adam, Abram, **Daud**, and **Yusef**. The Arabs were not dispersed into the nations, and have **preserved Hebrew words** well. What happened to their worship practices is another issue entirely.

Yahusha cried out the first verse of Psalm 22,
"Ali, Ali, lama sabakthani?" in the Hebrew tongue. He did not say "Eli, Eli." How do we know? Because the Masoretes had not yet corrupted the vocalization with their made-up "niqqud" vowel-markings. This is another tradition we are freed from, removing a huge language barrier, if one's stronghold (thought prison, boxing in a person's understanding) will allow it. This translation is for the next, and possibly the **last** generation before Yahusha returns. The drought is ending; Living Water is now flowing.

"Then Yahuah will guide you continually, and satisfy your being in drought, and strengthen your bones. And you shall be like a watered garden, and like a spring of water, whose waters do not fail. And those from among you shall build the old waste places. You shall raise up the foundations of many generations. And you would be called the Repairer of the breach, the Restorer of streets to dwell in." (Isaiah) **YashaYahu** 58:11, 12

Here is the most revealing explanation of what has been going on:
"See, days are coming," declares the Master Yahuah, "that I shall send a hunger in the land, not a hunger for bread, nor a thirst for water, but for hearing the Words of Yahuah. And they shall wander from sea to sea, and from north to east – they shall diligently search, seeking the Word of Yahuah, but they shall not find it." – Amus 8:11, 12

The **Living Words** are able to be found among Yahusha's Natsarim. We are His Hekal (Temple, Dwelling Place, His body). **"He who has an ear, let him hear what the Ruach says to the assemblies."** Rev 2:7 The 7 annual festivals of Yahuah have not been understood by Christianity, nor the Yahudim that have faithfully observed them for thousands of years. This is another case of "whatever is concealed shall be revealed". This is the **first generation** that has comprehended the significance of these "shadows" of things to come for the body of Mashiak They are redemption shadows, depicting the work of redemption by Yahusha. There are 7 of them, and they are agricultural allegories to illustrate the deliverance of Yisharal: Passover, Matsah, First-fruits, Shabuoth, Yom Teruah, Yom Kaphar, and Sukkoth allow us to see dimly as in a mirror through our observance of these festivals. Festivals are abstractions, or metaphorical ideas about Yisharal's redemption.

Yahusha was born during Sukkoth (also known as Tents, Tabernacles) at

(BYNV tract, page 3 of 4)

Beth Lekem (house of bread). Shabuoth was being observed at Acts 2, a wedding anniversary of the marriage between Yahuah & Yisharal that occurred at Sinai, the giving of the Living Words, or Covenant. The marriage Covenant is spoken of by Stephen at Acts 7. He uttered the Name aloud and was stoned for it. Hebrew roots are uniform in the reader's mind in this translation.

"Besorah" is equivalent to the Greek word *EUANGELION* (G2098) which became transformed into a newly created word, *GOSPEL* (god+spel). When you read the word "gospel" in your old versions, it is really the Hebrew word **besorah**: message. *The objective is to make this the best translation for the next generation of Yahusha's followers. You will be delighted to see the new improvements, such as how "the apple of My eye" is rendered. The world inherited this from the* KJV. AUTHORIZED VERSION

The Hebrew word, *ishon* (little-man of the eye), is not a fruit, or "apple." This was first used in the **KJV**, 1611.

The Hebrew idiom can be rendered several ways, but *apple* would not be the most appropriate. It relates to the popularized myth that the **fruit of temptation** was an apple. The KJV was made by Anglican Catholics using the Latin Vulgate. No apples are involved in either case.

The abstract meaning, rather than the literal meaning, points to the object of our **affections**, something highly valued we fix our attention on. The BYNV translates this Hebrew word **treasure** as informed by the context (surrounding sentences). This idea of *treasure* illuminates the words of Yahusha, and how it relates to the "ishon," or little man of the eye:

"For where your **treasure** is, there your **heart** shall be also. [see Proverbs 7:1,2 below] "The lamp of the body is the **eye**. If therefore your eye is good, all your body shall be enlightened." Mt. 6:21

You can see that Yahusha was involved in this translation, just from making this connection between eye, treasure, and the Hebrew word ishon.

"My son, guard my words, And treasure up My commands with you. Guard my commands and live, And My Torah as the treasure of your eye."

Are we the apple, or the treasure of His eye? Does your version copy the Anglican Catholic KJV, A direct translation from the Catholic Latin Vulgate?

Google: BYNV

You can get the Kindle Version in seconds:

The soft cover is a 6" x 9" paperback. The deluxe cover edition has smyth-sewn pages and a white ribbon. Available by phone or online ordering:

(BYNV tract, page 4 of 4)

The four pages above are from a downloadable PDF you can obtain for free at www.torahzone.net

1 Korinthians 13:1-13 describes love for us:

"If I speak with the tongues of men and of messengers, but do not have love, I have become as sounding brass or a clanging cymbal. And if I have prophecy, and know all secrets and all knowledge, and if I have all belief, so as to remove mountains, but do not have love, I am none at all. And if I give out all my possessions to feed the poor, and if I give my body to be burned, but do not have love, I am not profited at all. Love is patient, is kind, love does not envy, love does not boast, is not puffed up, does not behave indecently, does not seek its own, is not provoked, reckons not the evil, does not rejoice over the disobedience, but rejoices in the truth, it covers all, believes all, expects all, endures all. Love never fails.

And whether there be prophecies, they shall be inactive; or tongues, they shall cease; or knowledge, it shall be inactive. For we know in part and we prophesy in part. But when that which is perfect has come, then that which is in part shall be inactive. When I was a child, I spoke as a child, I thought as a child, I reasoned as a child.

But when I became a man, I did away with childish things. For now we see in a mirror, dimly, but then face to face. Now I know in part, but then I shall know, as I also have been known. And now belief, expectation, and love remain – these three; but the greatest of these is love."

"The heaven and the arets shall pass away, but My Words shall by no means pass away." Mt. 24:35 – BYNV

45

"Do not think that I came to destroy the Turah or the Prophets. I did not come to destroy but to complete. For truly, I say to you, till the heaven and the arets pass away, one yod or one tittle shall by no means pass from the Turah till all be done. Whoever, then, breaks one of the least of these commands, and teaches men so, shall be called least in the reign of the shamayim; but whoever does and teaches them, he shall be called great in the reign of the shamayim." Mt. 5:17-19 BYNV

Teach all nations the Name, and to obey all we were commanded to obey. The traditions of men have been inherited from our fathers, and are futility. The Torah has been abandoned, and the way of Truth has been considered to be evil (2 Peter 2:2). If we abide in Yahusha's Word, we are truly His followers.

He said, *"I am the Vine, you are the Natsarim."* Yahuah is Yahusha, and the Natsarim are saying,

"Baruk haba bashem Yahuah."

If you have learned anything helpful from this book, please check out my author's page at *amazon.com*:

BYNV - in print as 2 separate books - less bulky

BYNV VOLUME ONE
BARASHITH - YEKEZQAL

BYNV VOLUME TWO
HUSHA - REVELATION

NOTES

LETTER CHART

	HEBREW	ARAMAIC			GREEK		LATIN
alef	⟨	א	1	ox	alpha	A	A
beth	⟨	ב	2	house	beta	B	B
gimel	⟨	ג	3	camel	gamma	Γ	G
daleth	⟨	ד	4	door	delta	Δ	D
hay	⟨	ה	5	window	hoi	H	H
uau	Y	ו	6	hook	**upsilon**	Y	U
zayin	⟨	ז	7	weapon	zeta	Z	Z
heth	H	ח	8	fence	(h)eta	H	CH
teth	⊗	ט	9	winding	theta	Θ	T
yod	⟨	'	10	hand	iota	I	Y
kaph	⟨	כ	20	bent hand	kappa	K	K
lamed	⟨	ל	30	goad	lambda	Λ	L
mem	⟨	מ	40	water	mu	M	M
nun	⟨	נ	50	fish	nu	N	N
samek	⟨	ס	60	prop	xei	Ξ	S
ayin	O	ע	70	eye	omega	Ω	E/A
pe	⟨	פ	80	mouth	pei	Π	P
tsadee	⟨	צ	90	hook	zeta	Z	TS
koph	⟨	ק	100	needle eye	chi	X	Q
resh	⟨	ר	200	head	rho	P	R
shin	W	ש	300	tooth	sigma	Σ	SH
tau	X	ת	400	mark	tau	T	T

48

Made in the USA
Las Vegas, NV
18 December 2024

14641873R00030